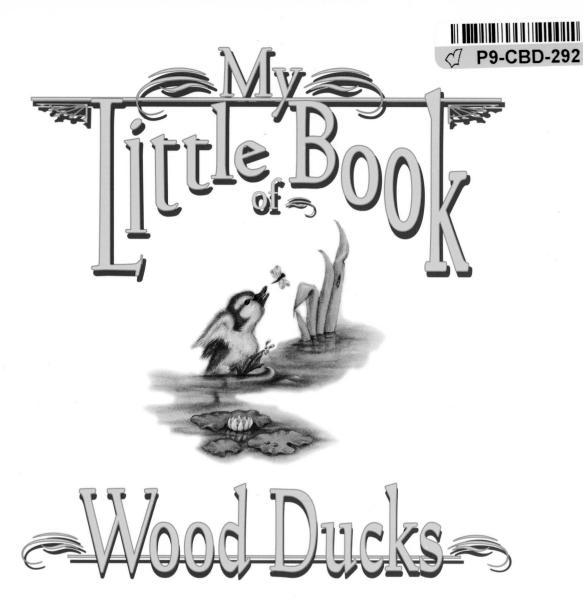

My Little Book of Wood Ducks

By Hope Irvin Marston
Illustrated by Maria Magdalena Brown

NORTHWORD PRESS
Minnetonka, Minnesota

Two wood ducks flitted in and out
of the treetops at the edge
of the forest.

They were searching for a safe place
to make their nest.

SWISH!
The female landed
on a branch.

She squeezed into a
rotted woodpecker hole
in a big, old oak tree.

A gray squirrel that once lived there had left a bed of leaves.

The wood duck sat down and turned around. The nest was just right.

She stretched and fluffed her feathers. As she preened herself, a few downy feathers fell out. The duck settled in her new home.

Each day for nine days
the mother wood duck
laid one whitish egg
in her nest.

She covered the eggs
with soft feathers
to keep them warm
when she and her mate
were away. And to hide
them from hungry snakes.

One day the wood duck heard
a strange sound.

SCRITCH - SCRATCH!
SCRITCH - SCRATCH!
SCRITCH - SCRATCH!

Something was climbing up her
tree. She made sure her eggs were
safely tucked beneath her. Then
she peeked out. A raccoon was
crawling up the trunk
looking for lunch.

When he saw her, he
backed down.

The next day while the wood ducks were feeding at the pond, the raccoon climbed the tree again.

He slipped away when he could not reach the eggs.

The mother duck sat
on her nest for twenty-
eight days. Inside the
eggs, the ducklings began
to grow. Their mother
listened for sounds from
the shells.

When she got hungry,
she covered the eggs
with down.

Then she flew to the pond
to catch tadpoles, insects and
minnows with her mate.

On the thirtieth day
she heard a new sound.
"Peep! Peep!"
The first egg had hatched.
Her waiting was over.

One by one the tiny wood ducks pipped their way out of their shells. Soon nine ducklings crowded the nest. Their mother kept them warm. In a few hours the lively little babies were covered with fluffy down.

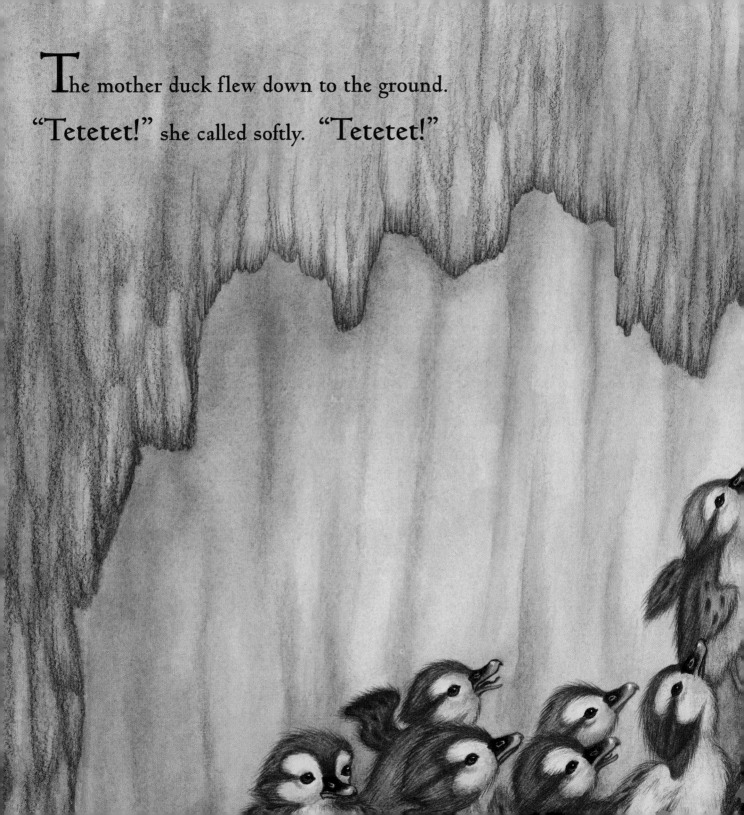

The mother duck flew down to the ground.
"Tetetet!" she called softly. "Tetetet!"

Her babies heard her.

With their tiny claws, they scrambled up to the opening of their nest. Then they threw themselves out and dropped to the ground.

Their soft, downy coats kept them from getting hurt.

The nine little wood ducks trailed single file after their mother to the pond.

Suddenly a dark
cloud appeared
above them.

It was a hawk.

"HOE-EEK! HOE-EEK!" cried the mother duck.
She and her babies scurried under cover to hide. Later, the wood
duck hurried her ducklings to the water.

"Kuk, kuk, kuk, kuk, kuk," she called as she slid in.
The ducklings waded in and swam after her. From
now on they would live
on the pond.

The mother duck began teaching her babies
how to catch insects. And tadpoles. And minnows.

"HOE-EEK! HOE-EEK!"
the mother duck called.

A snapping turtle was swimming
toward the ducklings.

SPLASH!

Nine tiny
ducklings dived
and scattered.
The turtle
could not
catch them.

When it was safe, the ducklings paddled back to their mother.

All morning they explored their new home.

Later the mother duck led them to the shore
to rest. One. Two. Three. Four. Five. Six.
Seven. Eight. Nine.

Then the ducklings tucked their
heads under their wings and
went to sleep.

When they awakened, they were hungry. They pecked at the acorns and the beechnuts on the ground. Then they scooted back into the water.

"HOE-EEK!
HOE-EEK!"
A muskrat was heading
toward the ducklings. They
swam to shore and hid
in the undergrowth.

Soon they would lose their
baby feathers and grow
flying feathers.

One day they would fly away to
build nests and start their
own families.

But for now, they snuggle
against their mother and
go to sleep.

DEDICATION
To Kim and Jen-Jen

NORTH**W**ORD PRESS
5900 Green Oak Drive
Minnetonka, MN 55343

ISBN 1-55971-467-0

Designed by Amy J. Monday

For a free catalog describing NorthWord's line of books and gift items, call toll free 1-800-336-5666

Library of Congress Cataloging-in-Publication Data
Marston, Hope Irvin.
    My little book of wood ducks / by Hope Irvin Marston;
illustrations by Maria Magdalena Brown.
        p. cm.
    ISBN 1-55971-467-0
    1. Wood duck—Juvenile literatu   Ducks.]
    I. Brown, Maria Magdalena, ill.
II. Title.
QL696.A52M37 1995
598.4'1—dc20   94-40917
                                      CIP
                                              AC

Printed in Canada.